W9-CCC-988

perfect waffles

FOG CITY PRESS

Published by Fog City Press
415 Jackson Street, Suite 200
San Francisco, CA 94111 USA

© 2008 Weldon Owen Inc.

Executive Chairman, Weldon Owen Group **John Owen**
CEO and President, Weldon Owen Inc. **Terry Newell**
Senior VP, International Sales **Stuart Laurence**
VP, Sales and New Business Development **Amy Kaneko**

VP and Publisher **Roger Shaw**
Managing Editor, Fog City Press **Karen Perez**
Project Editor **Norman Kolpas**

VP and Creative Director **Gaye Allen**
Art Director **Heather Stewart**
Project Designer **Jason Budow**

Photography **Carin Krasner**
Food Styling **Karen Gillingham**

Production Director **Chris Hemesath**
Production Manager **Michelle Duggan**
Color Manager **Teri Bell**

ISBN-10: 1-74089-781-1
ISBN-13: 978-1-740897-81-5

First Printed 2008
10 9 8 7 6 5 4 3 2 1

Color separations by Bright Arts, Hong Kong
Printed in China by SNP-Leefung Printers Ltd.

A Weldon Owen Production

CONTENTS

introduction

Waffles are so widely loved and so varied that perfection is a matter of personal taste.

Do you prefer old-fashioned diner breakfast favorites, golden-brown on the outside and tender within, dripping with warm syrup and melted butter? Or do you go for tall, crispy Belgian-style waffles? Are you intrigued by the way some of today's hottest chefs use waffles in creative savory dishes for brunch, lunch, dinner, or even the cocktail hour? Or do you love waffles for dessert, maybe topped with ice cream and a sweet sauce?

Whatever your preference in waffles, this book offers satisfaction galore, with 35 delicious recipes for waffles and toppings both sweet and savory. Every one of them has been kitchen-tested to deliver excellent results with today's easy-to-use electric waffle irons, from classic round or square waffles to tall Belgian waffles to delightful "five-of-hearts" models that produce pretty heart-shaped waffles. Each recipe stands on its own, ready for you to cook. But it's also a good idea to read over the instruction booklet that comes with your machine, as well as consulting the brief basics on the opposite page, to help you ensure success.

So start heating up your iron and get ready to enjoy waffle perfection!

perfect waffle basics

So many people have waffles only when they eat out that preparing them at home can seem strange at first. Modern electric waffle irons, however, make the job easy. After you've tried a few recipes, the process will feel familiar and easy. Keep the following guidelines in mind to help you achieve great results:

● **Read the instructions.** Get to know your waffle iron. Review the manufacturer's instructions on preheating, buttering or spraying the grids, how much batter to use, and cleanup.

● **Feel free to change the shape and size.** While each recipe specifies a particular kind of waffle, and some irons have reversible plates, feel free to adapt the recipes to your own machine.

● **Be aware that yields may differ.** Each recipe includes approximate yields, which may differ from one machine to another. You may need to use a different quantity of batter for yours. Until you're sure of what works best for your machine, make notes to help you remember.

● **Spread batter with care.** Some batters flow; others need spreading. A narrow-bladed offset spatula, which looks like a slender pancake turner, works especially well.

● **Enjoy yourself.** That's the whole point of making waffles!

classic quick
breakfast waffles

When you think of waffles, these are probably what you imagine. They're light, crisp-crusted, and great with maple syrup, butter, or jam.

MAKES ABOUT 4 STANDARD SQUARE
OR ROUND WAFFLES

1 cup (5 oz/155 g) all-purpose (plain) flour

1 teaspoon baking powder

pinch of salt

1½ tablespoons sugar

1 cup (8 fl oz/250 ml) milk

1 large egg

2 tablespoons unsalted butter, melted

softened butter, maple syrup, jam, or fruit puree, for serving

crisp thick-cut bacon or mixed berries, for serving (optional)

- Preheat a standard square or round waffle iron. If you want to hold the waffles until serving time, preheat the oven to 200°F (95°C).

- In a large mixing bowl, whisk together the flour, baking powder, salt, and sugar. In another bowl, thoroughly whisk together the milk and egg. Pour the liquid ingredients over the dry ingredients and stir until just combined. Stir in the 2 tablespoons of melted butter.

- Lightly butter or spray the waffle iron's grids, if needed. (Brush or spray the grids again only if subsequent waffles stick.)

- Spoon out ½ cup (4 fl oz/125 ml) of batter (or the amount recommended by the waffle iron's manufacturer) onto the hot iron. Using a metal spatula or wooden spoon, smooth the batter to within ¼ inch (6 mm) of the edge. Close the lid and bake until browned and crisp. Serve the waffles immediately, or keep them, in a single layer, on a rack in the preheated oven while you make the rest of the batch.

- Serve with traditional toppings like butter, maple syrup, jam, or fruit puree. For a more leisurely meal, add some crisp bacon or berries.

cottage cheese and honey waffles

Just a few minutes of cooking transform the bumpy texture of cottage cheese into a creamy consistency complemented by a touch of honey.

MAKES ABOUT 6 STANDARD SQUARE
OR ROUND WAFFLES

1¾ cups (9 oz/280 g) all-purpose (plain) flour

2 teaspoons baking powder

¼ teaspoon baking soda (bicarbonate of soda)

½ teaspoon salt

1 cup (8 oz/250 g) cottage cheese

1 cup (8 fl oz/250 ml) milk

2 large eggs

2½ tablespoons honey

4 tablespoons (2 oz/60 g) unsalted butter, melted

Peach-Honey Sauce (page 18), for serving

- Preheat a standard square or round waffle iron. If you want to hold the waffles until serving time, preheat the oven to 200°F (95°C).

- In a medium mixing bowl, whisk together the flour, baking powder, baking soda, and salt. In a large bowl, thoroughly whisk together the cottage cheese, milk, eggs, and honey; don't worry if the cottage cheese curds remain. With a rubber spatula, gradually stir in the dry ingredients until just combined. Stir in the melted butter.

- Lightly butter or spray the waffle iron's grids, if needed. (Brush or spray the grids again only if subsequent waffles stick.)

- Spoon out ½ cup (4 fl oz/125 ml) of batter (or the amount recommended by the waffle iron's manufacturer) onto the hot iron. Using a metal spatula or wooden spoon, smooth the batter almost to the edge of the grids. Close the lid and bake until browned and crisp. Serve the waffles immediately, or keep them, in a single layer, on a rack in the preheated oven while you make the rest of the batch.

- Serve one or two waffles per person, passing the sauce at the table.

cornbread
waffles

Cornmeal lends waffles the sweetness, golden glow, and crisp crust people love in cornbread. Look for coarse stone-ground cornmeal.

MAKES ABOUT 6 STANDARD SQUARE OR ROUND WAFFLES

1 cup (5 oz/155 g) all-purpose (plain) flour

1 cup (5 oz/155 g) yellow cornmeal (polenta), preferably stone-ground

2 teaspoons baking powder

½ teaspoon baking soda (bicarbonate of soda)

¼ teaspoon salt

2 cups (16 fl oz/500 ml) buttermilk

¼ cup (2 fl oz/60 ml) maple syrup

2 large eggs

4 tablespoons (2 oz/60 g) unsalted butter, melted

maple syrup, for serving

Grand Marnier Oranges (page 18), for serving

- Preheat a standard square or round waffle iron. If you want to hold the waffles until serving time, preheat the oven to 200°F (95°C).

- In a large mixing bowl, whisk together the flour, cornmeal, baking powder, baking soda, and salt. In another bowl, thoroughly whisk together the buttermilk, maple syrup, and eggs. Pour the liquid ingredients over the dry ingredients and stir until just combined. Stir in the melted butter.

- Lightly butter or spray the waffle iron's grids, if needed. (Brush or spray the grids again only if subsequent waffles stick.)

- Spoon out ½ cup (4 fl oz/125 ml) of batter (or the amount recommended by the waffle iron's manufacturer) onto the hot iron. Using a metal spatula or wooden spoon, smooth the batter almost to the edge of the grids. Close the lid and bake until browned and crisp. Serve the waffles immediately, or keep them, in a single layer, on a rack in the preheated oven while you make the rest of the batch.

- Serve the waffles on warmed plates with lots of maple syrup; or top with Grand Marnier Oranges, removing the marinated orange segments from their container with a slotted spoon.

buckwheat and oatmeal
Belgian waffles

A little buckwheat flour lends an earthy taste to waffles. Here, oats, wheat germ, brown sugar, and almond extract round out the flavor.

¾ cup (4 oz/125 g) all-purpose (plain) flour

⅓ cup (1 oz/30 g) old-fashioned (rolled) oats

¼ cup (1 oz/30 g) buckwheat flour

2 tablespoons wheat germ

1 tablespoon baking powder

¼ teaspoon salt

3 tablespoons firmly packed light brown sugar

¼ cup (1 oz/30 g) chopped walnuts

grated zest of 1 orange

1½ cups (12 fl oz/375 ml) buttermilk

3 large eggs

¼ teaspoon almond extract

3 tablespoons (1½ oz/45 g) unsalted butter, melted

Orange Marmalade Butter (page 19), for serving

maple syrup, for serving

• Preheat a standard square or round waffle iron. If you want to hold the waffles until serving time, preheat the oven to 200°F (95°C).

• In a large mixing bowl, whisk together the all-purpose flour, oats, buckwheat flour, wheat germ, baking powder, salt, and sugar. Stir in the walnuts and orange zest. In another bowl, whisk together the buttermilk, eggs, and almond extract until thoroughly blended. Pour the liquid ingredients over the dry ingredients and stir with the whisk until just combined. Stir in the melted butter.

• Lightly butter or spray the waffle iron's grids, if needed. (Brush or spray the grids again only if subsequent waffles stick.)

• Spoon out ½ cup (4 fl oz/125 ml) of batter (or the amount recommended by the waffle iron's manufacturer) onto the hot iron. Using a metal spatula or wooden spoon, smooth the batter to within ¼ inch (6 mm) of the edge. Close the lid and bake until the underside of the waffle is browned; turn the waffle over and brown and crisp the other side. Serve immediately, or keep them, in a single layer, on a rack in the preheated oven while you make the rest of the batch. Stir the batter between each baking, since the oats and buckwheat tend to thicken the batter as it stands.

• Serve with Orange Marmalade Butter and pass syrup at the table.

whole-wheat
cinnamon-raisin waffles

These waffles will send an enticing cinnamony aroma throughout your home. They're exceptional served with plain or sweetened cream cheese.

MAKES ABOUT 5 STANDARD SQUARE
OR ROUND WAFFLES

1 cup (5 oz/155 g) all-purpose
(plain) flour

$2/3$ cup (4 oz/125 g) whole-wheat
(wholemeal) flour

1 tablespoon baking powder

$1/4$ teaspoon baking soda
(bicarbonate of soda)

$1/8$ teaspoon salt

$1 1/2$ teaspoons ground cinnamon

2 tablespoons firmly packed
light brown sugar

2 tablespoons granulated (white)
sugar

$1 3/4$ cups (14 fl oz/435 ml) buttermilk

$1/2$ teaspoon vanilla extract

2 large eggs

$3/4$ cup (3 oz/90 g) plump, moist raisins

4 tablespoons (2 oz/60 g) unsalted
butter, melted

Velvet Cream Cheese (page 19),
for serving

maple syrup, for serving

• Preheat a standard square or round waffle iron. If you want to hold the waffles until serving time, preheat the oven to 200°F (95°C).

• In a large mixing bowl, whisk together the flours, baking powder, baking soda, salt, and cinnamon. Whisk in both sugars. In another bowl, whisk together the buttermilk, vanilla, and eggs until thoroughly blended. Pour the liquid ingredients over the dry ingredients and stir with the whisk until just combined. Fold in the raisins and melted butter.

• Lightly butter or spray the waffle iron's grids, if needed. (Brush or spray the grids again only if subsequent waffles stick.)

• Spoon out $1/2$–$2/3$ cup (4–$5 1/2$ fl oz/125–165 ml) of batter (or the amount recommended by the waffle iron's manufacturer) onto the hot iron. Using a metal spatula or wooden spoon, smooth the batter to within $1/4$ inch (6 mm) of the edge. Close the lid and bake until browned and crisp. Serve the waffles immediately, or keep them, in a single layer, on a rack in the preheated oven while you make the rest of the batch.

• Put the waffles on warm plates and top with Velvet Cream Cheese, to be spread like butter. Pass maple syrup at the table to be poured over each waffle as desired.

oatmeal
and banana waffles

Think of these waffles as comfort food. Combining nutty oats, sweet bananas, and dessert spices, they're as pleasurable as pudding.

MAKES ABOUT 5 STANDARD SQUARE
OR ROUND WAFFLES

1 cup (3 oz/90 g) old-fashioned
(rolled—not instant) oats

1 cup (5 oz/150 g) all-purpose
(plain) flour

1 tablespoon baking powder

½ teaspoon baking soda
(bicarbonate of soda)

¼ teaspoon ground cinnamon

pinch ground nutmeg

3 tablespoons firmly packed
dark brown sugar

1½ cups (12 oz/375 ml) buttermilk

2 large eggs

2 ripe bananas, thinly sliced

4 tablespoons (2 oz/60 g)
unsalted butter, melted

maple syrup, honey, and melted butter,
for serving

• Preheat a standard square or round waffle iron. If you want to hold the waffles until serving time, preheat the oven to 200°F (95°C).

• In a large mixing bowl, whisk together the oats, flour, baking powder, baking soda, spices, and sugar. In another bowl, whisk together the buttermilk and eggs until thoroughly blended. Pour the liquid ingredients over the dry ingredients and stir with the whisk until just combined. Fold in the banana slices and melted butter.

• Lightly butter or spray the waffle iron's grids, if needed. (Brush or spray the grids again only if subsequent waffles stick.)

• Spoon out ½–⅔ cup (4–5½ fl oz/125–165 ml) of batter (or the amount recommended by the waffle iron's manufacturer) onto the hot iron. Using a metal spatula or wooden spoon, push the thick batter up to the edge. Close the lid and bake until golden and crisp. (It may take a little longer than other waffles.) Serve the waffles immediately, or keep them, in a single layer, on a rack in the preheated oven while you make the rest of the batch. Stir the batter between batches to redistribute the banana.

• Put the waffles on warm plates and pass maple syrup, honey, and melted butter at the table to be added as desired.

smoked salmon waffles
with dill and onion

An elegant brunch alternative to bagels with lox and cream cheese, these rich waffles are elegant enough to serve with Champagne.

MAKES ABOUT 6 STANDARD SQUARE
OR ROUND WAFFLES

1¾ cups (9 oz/280 g) all-purpose (plain) flour

2 teaspoons baking powder

1 teaspoon salt

¼ teaspoon black pepper

2 cups (16 fl oz/500 ml) milk

2 large eggs

3 oz (90 g) Nova Scotia–style smoked salmon, finely chopped

1 medium red (Spanish) onion, peeled and finely diced

¼ cup (½ oz/15 g) snipped fresh dill

4 tablespoons (2 oz/60 g) unsalted butter, melted

softened cream cheese and finely chopped dill; or crème fraîche (or sour cream) and salmon caviar, for serving

• Preheat a standard square or round waffle iron. If you want to hold the waffles until serving time, preheat the oven to 200°F (95°C).

• In a large mixing bowl, whisk together the flour, baking powder, salt, and pepper. In another bowl, whisk together the milk and eggs until thoroughly blended. Pour the liquid ingredients over the dry ingredients and stir with the whisk until just combined. Fold in the salmon, onion, dill, and melted butter.

• Lightly butter or spray the waffle iron's grids, if needed. (Brush or spray the grids again only if subsequent waffles stick.)

• Spoon out ½ cup (4 fl oz/125 ml) of batter (or the amount recommended by the waffle iron's manufacturer) onto the hot iron. Using a metal spatula or wooden spoon, spread the batter evenly over the grids, stopping right before the edge. Close the lid and bake until golden and crisp. Serve the waffles immediately, or keep them, in a single layer, on a rack in the preheated oven while you make the rest of the batch.

• Put the waffles on warm plates and top with either a scoop of cream cheese and a sprinkling of chopped dill or, for a special occasion, a generous spoonful of crème fraîche (or sour cream) and some salmon caviar.

peanut butter
and jelly waffles

The peanut butter flavor is unmistakable in these golden waffles, which are lightened by whipped egg whites folded into the batter.

MAKES ABOUT 8 BELGIAN WAFFLES

1¼ cups (6½ oz/190 g) all-purpose (plain) flour

1 tablespoon baking powder

¼ teaspoon baking soda (bicarbonate of soda)

¼ teaspoon ground cinnamon

3 tablespoons sugar

⅓ cup (3 fl oz/90 ml) crunchy peanut butter

2 large eggs, separated

1¼ cups (10 fl oz/310 ml) milk

3 tablespoons unsalted butter, melted

jelly or jam, for topping

● Preheat a Belgian waffle iron. If you want to hold the waffles until serving time, preheat the oven to 200°F (95°C).

● In a medium mixing bowl, whisk together the flour, baking powder, baking soda, cinnamon, and sugar. In a large mixing bowl, use a rubber spatula to cream together the peanut butter and egg yolks. Add about ½ cup (125 ml) of the milk and mix it in with the spatula, pressing against the side of the bowl, to achieve a lumpy but fluid consistency. Stir in the rest of the milk. Add the dry ingredients to the liquid ingredients and stir until just combined. Fold in the melted butter. In a clean dry bowl, with clean dry beaters, beat the egg whites until stiff but not dry. Fold them into the batter.

● Lightly butter or spray the waffle iron's grids, if needed. (Brush or spray the grids again only if subsequent waffles stick.)

● Spoon out a generous ½ cup (4 fl oz/125 ml) of batter (or the amount recommended by the waffle iron's manufacturer) onto the hot iron. Using a metal spatula or wooden spoon, spread evenly over the grid up to the edge. Close the lid and bake until the waffle is a deep golden brown. Serve immediately, or keep, in a single layer, on a rack in the preheated oven while you make the rest of the batch.

● Fill each waffle square with some jam. Let the waffles cool, then refill squares in which the waffle has absorbed the jam.

peach-honey sauce

MAKES ABOUT ABOUT 3 CUPS
(24 FL OZ/750 ML)

12 medium-sized ripe peaches

juice of 1 lemon (or more to taste)

2 tablespoons honey
(or more to taste)

- Bring 1 quart (1 l) of water to a boil in a medium-sized saucepan. Add the peaches and keep them submerged for 10–15 seconds. Remove with a slotted spoon and, when cool enough to handle, slip off the skins.

- Cut the peaches into small pieces. Put the pieces into a blender or food processor with the lemon juice and honey. Blend or process until smoothly pureed. Taste and, if needed, add more lemon juice or honey. Transfer to a tightly covered container and refrigerate for up to 3 days.

Grand Marnier oranges

MAKES ABOUT ABOUT 3 CUPS
(24 FL OZ/750 ML)

3 large, juicy oranges

1 to 2 teaspoons sugar

2 teaspoons Grand Marnier or other orange liqueur

- With a small, sharp knife, peel the oranges, cutting off the peel thickly enough to remove the white pith and expose the fruit's juicy pulp.

- Working over a nonreactive bowl, cut between each orange segment so that the segment, minus the connecting membrane, drops into the bowl. When you've cut all the segments, squeeze the juice from the remaining membranes into the bowl; discard the membranes. With a spoon, pick out and discard any seeds that may have fallen into the bowl.

- Stir in the sugar, adjusting the amount to your taste and to the sweetness of the oranges. Stir in the Grand Marnier. Cover the bowl and set aside or refrigerate until serving time.

orange marmalade butter

MAKES ABOUT ABOUT ¾ CUP
(6 OZ/185 G)

½ cup (4 oz/125 g) unsalted butter,
softened

¼ cup (2¾ oz/80 g) orange
marmalade

- Put the butter and marmalade in a small mixing bowl or in the work bowl of a mini food processor. Beat them together with a hand-held electric mixer on medium speed, or process them, until well blended.

- If not using right away, turn out the orange butter onto a piece of plastic wrap. Using the wrap as a guide, roll the butter into a log. Seal the edges of the log with the excess plastic wrap. Refrigerate until needed. The log can stay in the refrigerator for 1 week or the freezer for up to 1 month.

velvet cream cheese

MAKES ABOUT ABOUT ½ CUP
(4 OZ/125 G)

3 oz (90 g) cream cheese, softened

2 tablespoons heavy (double) cream

1½ teaspoons ground cinnamon

1 teaspoon sugar (or more to taste)

- Put the cream cheese and cream in a small mixing bowl and beat with a whisk or a hand-held electric mixer on low speed until blended. Beat in the cinnamon and the sugar to taste.

- Cover and refrigerate until needed. (The spread keeps for up to 5 days.)

ham, pepper, and onion waffles

Just like that diner mainstay, the Western omelet, these waffles artfully meld the flavors of ham, sweet peppers, and onion.

MAKES ABOUT 4 STANDARD SQUARE
OR ROUND WAFFLES

4 tablespoons (2 oz/60 g)
unsalted butter

½ green bell pepper (capsicum),
seeded and cut into small dice

½ red bell pepper (capsicum),
seeded and cut into small dice

1 small yellow onion, chopped

¼ pound (125 g) fully cooked ham or
Canadian bacon, cut into small cubes

1¾ cups (9 oz/280 g) all-purpose
(plain) flour

1 tablespoon baking powder

⅛ teaspoon salt

⅛ teaspoon black pepper

2 cups (16 fl oz/500 ml) milk

2 large eggs

hot pepper sauce (such as Tabasco),
to taste

Spicy Tomato Sauce (page 26),
for serving

• Melt the butter in a medium skillet over medium heat. Add the bell peppers and onion and sauté until they soften slightly, 3–4 minutes. Stir in the ham. Remove from the heat.

• Preheat a standard square or round waffle iron. If you want to hold the waffles until serving time, preheat the oven to 200°F (95°C).

• In a large mixing bowl, whisk together the flour, baking powder, salt, and pepper. In another bowl, whisk together the milk and eggs. Add hot pepper sauce to taste; beat again. Pour the liquid ingredients over the dry ingredients and stir with the whisk until just combined. Fold in the vegetables and ham.

• Lightly butter or spray the waffle iron's grids, if needed. (Brush or spray the grids again only if subsequent waffles stick.)

• Spoon out ½ cup (4 fl oz/125 ml) of batter (or the amount recommended by the waffle iron's manufacturer) onto the hot iron. Using a metal spatula or wooden spoon, spread the batter evenly. Close the lid and bake until lightly golden and set. Serve immediately, or keep them, in a single layer, on a rack in the preheated oven while you make the rest. Stir the batter between batches.

• Reheat the Spicy Tomato Sauce, if necessary, and adjust the seasonings. Serve the waffles on warmed plates with the sauce.

golden polenta
waffles

These waffles turn out fluffy, finely textured, and subtle, deliciously straddling the line between posh food and peasant fare.

MAKES ABOUT 4 STANDARD SQUARE OR ROUND WAFFLES

2 cups water (16 fl oz/500 ml)

1 teaspoon coarse salt

4 tablespoons (2 oz/60 g) unsalted butter

⅓ cup (2½ oz/75 g) yellow cornmeal (polenta), preferably stone-ground

2 large eggs

½ cup (2½ oz/75 g) all-purpose (plain) flour

1 teaspoon baking powder

Creamy Goat Cheese Sauce (page 26), for serving

fresh herbs, for garnish

- To make the polenta, put the water, salt, and butter in a 2-quart (2-l) saucepan and bring to a boil over medium-high heat. Reduce the heat to low and, while stirring constantly with a wooden spoon, slowly pour in the cornmeal. Continue to stir over low heat until thick, smooth, and shiny, about 15 minutes. Pour into a large bowl.

- Preheat a standard square or round waffle iron. If you want to hold the waffles until serving time, preheat the oven to 200°F (95°C).

- One at time, beat the eggs into the polenta with a whisk. In a small bowl, whisk together the flour and baking powder, then sprinkle over the polenta and fold them in.

- Lightly butter or spray the waffle iron's grids, if needed. (Brush or spray the grids again only if subsequent waffles stick.)

- Spoon out ½ cup (4 fl oz/125 ml) of batter (or the amount recommended by the waffle iron's manufacturer) onto the hot iron. Using a metal spatula or wooden spoon, spread the batter evenly. Close the lid and bake until the waffle is honey brown and set. Serve the waffles immediately, or keep them, in a single layer, on a rack in the preheated oven while you make the rest.

- Place each waffle on a warmed serving plate. Spoon some Creamy Goat Cheese Sauce on top and garnish with fresh herbs.

shredded zucchini and cheddar cheese waffles

Full-bodied and flavorful, these waffles highlight the surprisingly subtle taste of shredded zucchini. An ideal dish for a casual lunch.

MAKES ABOUT 4 STANDARD SQUARE
OR ROUND WAFFLES

⅓ cup (3 fl oz/90 ml) extra-virgin
olive oil

1 large shallot, finely chopped

1 large clove garlic, finely chopped

1¼ cups (10 fl oz/310 ml) buttermilk

2 large eggs

1¼ cups (6½ oz/190 g) all-purpose
(plain) flour

2 teaspoons baking powder

¼ teaspoon baking soda
(bicarbonate of soda)

¾ teaspoon salt

¼ teaspoon black pepper

⅛ teaspoon ground nutmeg

1 small zucchini (courgette), about
8 oz (250 g), scrubbed but not peeled

¼ lb (4 oz/125 g) sharp
Cheddar cheese

plain yogurt or sour cream, for topping

• Warm the olive oil in a small, heavy skillet over very low heat. Add the shallot and garlic and stir just until fragrant, about 1 minute. Remove from the stove and cool briefly. Meanwhile, in a medium mixing bowl, whisk together the buttermilk and eggs. Whisk in the garlic and shallot. Set aside.

• Preheat a standard square or round waffle iron. If you want to hold the waffles until serving time, preheat the oven to 200°F (95°C).

• In a large mixing bowl, whisk together the flour, baking powder, baking soda, salt, pepper, and nutmeg. Shred (grate) the zucchini and Cheddar into the bowl. Mix with a rubber spatula. Pour the liquid ingredients over the dry ingredients and stir until just combined.

• Lightly butter or spray the waffle iron's grids, if needed. (Brush or spray the grids again only if subsequent waffles stick.)

• Spoon out ¾ cup (6 fl oz/185 ml) of batter (or slightly more than the amount recommended by the waffle iron's manufacturer) onto the hot iron. Using a metal spatula or wooden spoon, spread the batter evenly almost to the edge of the grids. Close the lid and bake until browned and crisp. Serve immediately, or keep the waffles, in a single layer, on a rack in the preheated oven while you make the rest.

• Place on warmed serving plates. Top with yogurt or sour cream.

spicy tomato sauce

MAKES ABOUT 1 CUP (8 FL OZ/250 ML)

1½ cups (12 oz/375 g) canned crushed tomatoes

¼ cup (2 fl oz/60 ml) water

3 tablespoons bottled chili sauce

hot pepper sauce (such as Tabasco), to taste

Worcestershire sauce, to taste

• Put the tomatoes, water, and chili sauce in a medium saucepan and bring to a boil over medium heat. Reduce the heat and simmer for 10 minutes, stirring occasionally. Season to taste with hot pepper sauce and Worcestershire sauce and set aside.

• The sauce can be made up to 3 days ahead and refrigerated.

creamy goat cheese sauce

MAKES ABOUT 1½ CUPS (12 FL OZ/375 ML)

6 oz (185 g) fresh soft goat cheese

¾ cup (6 fl oz/185 ml) milk

salt

white pepper

herbes de Provence (optional)

• Put the goat cheese and milk in the top of a double boiler placed over but not touching simmering water. Cook over medium heat, stirring, until the cheese melts and the mixture is smooth. Be careful not to overcook; too much heat can curdle the mixture. Stir in a little salt, white pepper, and herbes de Provence to taste. The sauce is ready to serve as soon as the mixture is melted and creamy.

• To make the sauce ahead, remove it from the double boiler, cool, and refrigerate, covered, until needed. Reheat in the double boiler.

garlic and basil sauce

MAKES ABOUT 2 CUPS (8 FL OZ/500 ML)

2 cups (4 oz/125 g) packed fresh
basil leaves

1 teaspoon salt, or more to taste

2 garlic cloves, peeled and sliced

¾ cup (6 fl oz/185 ml) extra-virgin
olive oil

- Put the basil, salt, garlic, and olive oil in a food processor or a blender and process until smooth, scraping down the sides of the bowl as needed.

- The sauce can be made up to 1 week in advance, covered tightly, and stored in the refrigerator. It can be frozen for up to 2 months.

grilled red pepper strips

MAKES ABOUT 3 CUPS
(24 FL OZ/750 ML)

6 large firm red bell peppers
(capsicums)

¾ cup (6 fl oz/185 ml) extra-virgin
olive oil

coarse salt

black pepper

1 to 2 large garlic cloves, peeled and
very finely sliced (optional)

¼ cup (½ oz/15 g) fresh basil leaves

- Working with one pepper at a time, impale it on the tines of a long-handled fork and hold it over a gas flame on the stovetop; or place it directly on the heating element of an electric range. Turn often to char its skin deeply and evenly. Place in a paper bag, close the bag, and continue with the rest of the peppers. After the last pepper has been charred, leave all the peppers in the bag to steam and cool for about 10 minutes. When the peppers are cool enough to handle, remove them from the bag and, with your fingers, peel off and discard the charred skins.

- Cut the peppers in half and remove and discard their stems, seeds, and veins. With a sharp knife, cut the peppers lengthwise into strips. Place the strips in a medium bowl. Add the olive oil and salt and pepper to taste and toss well. If you like, add the garlic to taste and toss again.

- At serving time, cut the basil leaves into long, thin strips and stir them in.

corn tortilla
waffle chips

Masa harina, the fine cornmeal flour used for making corn tortillas, gives these crunchy hors-d'oeuvre waffles their distinctive flavor.

MAKES ABOUT 4 FULL
FIVE-OF-HEARTS WAFFLES

½ cup (2½ oz/75 g) masa harina (corn tortilla flour)

½ cup (2½ oz/75 g) all-purpose (plain) flour

1¼ teaspoons baking powder

½ teaspoon salt

⅛ teaspoon black pepper

pinch cayenne pepper

1 cup (8 fl oz/250 ml) milk

1 large egg

2 tablespoons corn oil

Confetti Guacamole (page 36)

• Preheat a heart-shaped waffle iron. If you want to hold the waffles until serving time or to crisp them, preheat the oven to 200°F (95°C).

• In a large mixing bowl, whisk together the masa harina, flour, baking powder, salt, pepper, and cayenne. In another bowl, whisk together the milk and egg. Pour the liquid ingredients over the dry ingredients and whisk until just mixed. Fold in the corn oil.

• Lightly butter or spray the waffle iron's grids, if needed. (Brush or spray the grids again only if subsequent waffles stick.)

• Spoon out ½ cup (4 fl oz/125 ml) of batter (or the amount recommended by the waffle iron's manufacturer) onto the hot iron. Using a metal spatula or wooden spoon, spread the batter evenly over the grids. Close the lid and bake until the waffle is deep golden and crisped. Cut the waffle into hearts and place, in a single layer, on a rack in the preheated oven; continue making the remaining waffles.

• Bake the waffles for 1 hour, until they resemble crackers. Transfer to a cooling rack and cool to room temperature. (The waffles can be made up to 3 days ahead and stored in a loosely covered tin.)

• Pile the waffle chips on a platter. Put the guacamole in a bowl nearby so guests can spoon some on their chips.

fresh corn and sweet pepper waffles

The corn kernels speckling these light-crusted, pliable waffles retain their slight crunchiness and full summery sweetness.

MAKES ABOUT 6 FULL
FIVE-OF-HEARTS WAFFLES

2 ears fresh sweet corn, husked, kernels cut from the cobs

1 red bell pepper (capsicum), seeded and finely diced

½ jalapeño chile, seeded, deveined, and minced

1 cup (5 oz/155 g) all-purpose (plain) flour

½ cup (2½ oz/75 g) yellow cornmeal (polenta)

2 teaspoons baking powder

½ teaspoon baking soda (bicarbonate of soda)

½ teaspoon salt

¼ teaspoon black pepper

pinch cayenne pepper (optional)

pinch chili powder (optional)

1½ cups (12 fl oz/375 ml) buttermilk

2 large eggs

4 tablespoons (2 oz/60 g) unsalted butter, melted

Corn and Pepper Salsa (page 37)

- Preheat a heart-shaped waffle iron. If you want to hold the waffles until serving time, preheat the oven to 200°F (95°C).

- Put the corn kernels in a bowl and add the diced red pepper and jalapeño; set aside. In a large mixing bowl, whisk together the flour, cornmeal, baking powder, baking soda, salt, pepper, and, for slightly spicier results, the cayenne and chili powder. In another bowl, whisk together the buttermilk and eggs. Pour the liquid ingredients over the dry ingredients and whisk just until combined. Stir in the reserved corn mixture and the melted butter.

- Lightly butter or spray the waffle iron's grids, if needed. (Brush or spray the grids again only if subsequent waffles stick.)

- Spoon out a full ½ cup (4 fl oz/125 ml) of batter (or the amount recommended by the waffle iron's manufacturer) onto the hot iron. Using a metal spatula or wooden spoon, spread the thick batter evenly over the grids. Close the lid and bake until lightly golden and crisp. Remove the waffle and cut into hearts. Then, transfer to a cooling rack to serve at room temperature; or keep them warm in the preheated oven while you make the rest.

- Arrange the waffles on a platter and serve with the salsa.

blue corn chip
waffles

Blue corn is the original type of corn that was grown by Native Americans. Wonderfully earthy, it turns deep brown when baked in a waffle iron.

MAKES ABOUT 4 FULL
FIVE-OF-HEARTS WAFFLES

½ cup (2½ oz/75 g) blue cornmeal

½ cup (2½ oz/75 g) all-purpose (plain) flour

1 teaspoon baking powder

¼ teaspoon baking soda (bicarbonate of soda)

¼ teaspoon salt

¾ teaspoon chili powder

¼ teaspoon dried oregano

pinch ground cumin

1 cup (8 fl oz/250 ml) buttermilk

1 large egg

3 tablespoons corn oil

Confetti Guacamole (page 36) or Corn and Pepper Salsa (page 37)

• Preheat a heart-shaped waffle iron. If you want to hold the waffles until serving time, preheat the oven to 200°F (95°C).

• In a large mixing bowl, whisk together the blue cornmeal, flour, baking powder, baking soda, salt, chili powder, oregano, and cumin. In another bowl, whisk together the buttermilk and egg. Pour the liquid ingredients over the dry ingredients and whisk until just mixed. Fold in the corn oil.

• Lightly butter or spray the waffle iron's grids, if needed. (Brush or spray the grids again only if subsequent waffles stick.)

• Spoon out ½ cup (4 fl oz/125 ml) of batter (or the amount recommended by the waffle iron's manufacturer) onto the hot iron. Using a metal spatula or wooden spoon, spread the batter evenly over the grids. Close the lid and bake until the waffle is well browned and very crisp, giving it a little more time than you might other waffles. Transfer the crispy waffles, in a single layer, to a cooling rack and make the rest of the batch.

• Mound the waffle chips in a bowl. Put the guacamole or salsa alongside in another bowl and serve.

spiced couscous
waffles

Cinnamon, ginger, cumin, and turmeric give alluring flavor and color to couscous, the grainy Moroccan pasta featured in these waffles.

MAKES ABOUT 5 FULL
FIVE-OF-HEART WAFFLES

2 cups (16 fl oz/500 ml) chicken broth

3 tablespoons extra-virgin olive oil

1 teaspoon ground cinnamon

½ teaspoon ground ginger

½ teaspoon ground cumin

¼ teaspoon ground turmeric

½ cup (2½ oz/75 g) quick-cooking or instant couscous

1 large egg

1 cup (5 oz/150 g) all-purpose (plain) flour

2 teaspoons baking powder

½ teaspoon salt

Pepper and Olive Dip (page 36)

- In a medium saucepan, combine 1 cup (8 fl oz/250 ml) of the broth, 1 tablespoon of oil, and the spices. Bring to a boil over medium heat. Stirring continuously, slowly pour in the couscous. Reduce the heat to low and cook, stirring, for 1 minute. Remove from the heat, cover, and set aside until all the liquid is absorbed, about 5 minutes.

- Preheat a heart-shaped waffle iron. If you want to hold the waffles until serving time, preheat the oven to 200°F (95°C).

- Transfer the couscous to a large mixing bowl and stir with a fork to separate the grains. Whisk in the remaining 1 cup (8 fl oz/250 ml) of broth and the egg. In a small bowl, whisk together the flour, baking powder, and salt. Pour over the couscous and stir until mixed. Fold in the remaining 2 tablespoons oil.

- Lightly butter or spray the waffle iron's grids, if needed. (Brush or spray the grids again only if subsequent waffles stick.)

- Spoon out ½ cup (4 fl oz/125 ml) of batter (or the amount recommended by the waffle iron's manufacturer) onto the hot iron. Using a metal spatula or wooden spoon, spread the batter evenly over the grids. Close the lid and bake until the waffle is golden and the crust is firm. Serve immediately or keep the waffles, in a single layer, on a rack in the preheated oven while you make the rest.

- Put the dip in a bowl in the center of a platter and arrange the warm waffles around them for scooping and dipping.

parmesan and basil
waffle chips

The outstanding flavors in these waffles are Parmesan, olive oil, and fresh basil, making them ideal for a bruschetta-style presentation.

MAKES ABOUT 5 FULL
FIVE-OF-HEARTS WAFFLES

⅔ cup (3⅓ oz/100 g) all-purpose (plain) flour

⅓ cup (1⅔ oz/50 g) pasta flour (semolina flour)

1¼ teaspoons baking powder

¾ teaspoon salt

1¼ cups (10 fl oz/310 ml) milk

1 large egg

½ cup (1 oz/30 g) packed fresh basil leaves, shredded

¼ cup (1 oz/30 g) freshly grated Parmesan cheese

3 tablespoons extra-virgin olive oil

Balsamic-Marinated Tomatoes (page 37)

Fresh basil leaves, for garnish

- Preheat a heart-shaped waffle iron. If you want to hold the waffles until serving time, preheat the oven to 200°F (95°C).

- In a large mixing bowl, whisk together the flours, baking powder, and salt. In another bowl, whisk together the milk and egg. Pour the liquid ingredients over the dry ingredients and stir with the whisk until just combined. Fold in the basil, Parmesan, and olive oil.

- Lightly butter or spray the waffle iron's grids, if needed. (Brush or spray the grids again only if subsequent waffles stick.)

- Spoon out ½ cup (4 fl oz/125 ml) of batter (or the amount recommended by the waffle iron's manufacturer) onto the hot iron. Using a metal spatula or wooden spoon, smooth the batter. Close the lid and bake until lightly golden and set. Cut into serving-sized pieces and place, in a single layer, on a rack in the preheated oven while you make the rest of the batch. To crisp the waffles, continue baking for 1 hour. Transfer to a cooling rack and serve when they reach room temperature. (The waffle chips can be made up to 3 days ahead and stored at room temperature in a loosely covered tin.)

- Serve the chips with the Balsamic-Marinated Tomatoes passed in an attractive bowl with a spoon. Or arrange a few on individual plates, topping each with tomatoes and basil leaves.

confetti guacamole

MAKES ABOUT 2½ CUPS (20 FL OZ/625 ML)

3 plum (Roma) tomatoes

2 green (spring) onions

½ red bell pepper (capsicum)

½ jalapeño chile

½ teaspoon finely chopped garlic

½ lime, juiced, or more to taste

salt and black pepper

1 ripe avocado

1 tablespoon finely chopped fresh
cilantro (green coriander)

• Dice the tomatoes. Trim and thinly slice the white parts of the green onions. Seed, devein, and finely dice the bell pepper. Seed, devein, and mince the chile.

• Put the tomatoes, green onions, bell pepper, jalapeño, garlic, and lime juice in a nonreactive bowl and stir to mix, seasoning to taste with salt and pepper. Cover and refrigerate. (You can make this up to 2 hours ahead.)

• Just before serving, halve, pit, and peel the avocado and cut it into small cubes. Gently stir into the other ingredients, add the cilantro, and adjust the seasonings, if necessary, with a little more lime juice, salt, and pepper.

pepper and olive dip

MAKES 2 CUPS (16 FL OZ/500 ML)

1 (7-oz/210-g) jar roasted red peppers

1 large garlic clove, pressed

½ hot red chile pepper, minced

1 tablespoon extra-virgin olive oil

1 teaspoon tomato paste

salt and black pepper

1 cup (8 oz/250 g) cottage cheese

12 pitted brine-cured black olives

• Drain the peppers and pat them dry. Put all the ingredients except the cottage cheese and olives in the work bowl of a food processor or blender. Process until smooth, scraping down the sides of the container as necessary.

• Add the cottage cheese and continue to process until well blended and creamy. Add the olives and pulse several times to chop them and distribute them evenly through the mixture.

corn and pepper salsa

MAKES ABOUT 3 CUPS (750 ML)

1 to 2 ears fresh sweet corn

1½ red, green, or yellow bell
  peppers (capsicums)

½ jalapeño chile

3 green (spring) onions

1 lime, juiced

½ teaspoon salt

pinch chili powder

2 teaspoons corn oil or olive oil

1½ tablespoons minced fresh cilantro
(green coriander)

- Husk the corn and cut the kernels from the cobs. Seed, devein, and finely dice the bell peppers and the chile. Trim and thinly slice the white parts of the green onions.

- In a nonreactive bowl, toss the corn together with all of the other ingredients. Cover and refrigerate. (The salsa may be made up to 2 hours ahead.)

balsamic-marinated tomatoes

MAKES ABOUT 2½ CUPS
(20 FL OZ/60 ML)

4 large ripe tomatoes, halved, seeded,
and cut into small dice

1 to 2 cloves garlic, peeled
and finely chopped

2 tablespoons balsamic vinegar

1 tablespoon extra-virgin olive oil

- Put all the ingredients in a nonreactive medium bowl. Stir until thoroughly mixed. Serve within 20 minutes, before the tomatoes absorb too much of the dressing.

chocolate-amaretti
waffle cakes

Moist, cocoa-rich, and flecked with Italian macaroons and bittersweet chocolate, these are delicious on their own or with ice cream.

MAKES ABOUT 10 FULL
FIVE-OF-HEARTS WAFFLES

6 amaretti (Italian macaroons), from 3 large paper-wrapped individual-serving packets, plus extra

2 oz (60 g) bittersweet chocolate

1 1/4 cups (6 1/4 oz/190 g) all-purpose (plain) flour

1 1/2 teaspoons baking powder

1/4 teaspoon baking soda (bicarbonate of soda)

dash salt

3/4 cup (6 oz/185 g) sugar

1/3 cup (1 oz/30 g) cocoa powder

1 1/2 cups (12 fl oz/375 ml) milk

1 teaspoon vanilla extract

1/4 teaspoon almond extract

2 large eggs

1/3 cup (3 oz/90 g) unsalted butter, melted

confectioners' (icing) sugar, vanilla ice cream, and Hot Fudge Sauce (page 46), for serving

- Put the 6 amaretti and the chocolate in a food processor or a blender. Process just until the mixture is pulverized. Set aside.

- Preheat a heart-shaped waffle iron, and preheat the oven to 200°F (95°C).

- In a large mixing bowl, whisk together the flour, baking powder, baking soda, salt, sugar, and cocoa powder. In another bowl, whisk together the milk, vanilla, almond extract, and eggs. Pour the liquid ingredients over the dry ingredients and stir until just combined. Fold in the reserved amaretto-chocolate mixture and melted butter.

- Lightly butter or spray the waffle iron's grids, if needed. (Brush or spray the grids again only if subsequent waffles stick.)

- Spoon out 1/3 cup (3 fl oz/85 ml) of batter (or the amount recommended by the waffle iron's manufacturer) onto the hot iron. Using a metal spatula or wooden spoon, smooth the batter to within 1/4 inch (6 mm) of the edge. Close the lid and bake until just set, slightly less time than other waffles. Transfer to a cooling rack while you make the rest of the batch. Serve at room temperature; or warm briefly, about 2 minutes, in the preheated oven.

- Dust each waffle with confectioners' sugar. Top with ice cream, Hot Fudge Sauce, and crushed amaretti.

pumpkin pie waffles

Comforting and filling like pumpkin pie, these waffles feature the same sweet spices as that classic. If you like, garnish them with pecan pieces.

MAKES ABOUT 6 BELGIAN WAFFLES

1 cup (8 oz/250 g) pumpkin puree

½ cup (3½ oz/105 g) firmly packed dark brown sugar

¼ cup (2 oz/60 g) granulated (white) sugar

1½ teaspoons pumpkin pie spices

1¼ teaspoons grated fresh ginger

pinch salt

1⅓ cups (7 oz/220 g) all-purpose (plain) flour

1 tablespoon baking powder

½ teaspoon baking soda (bicarbonate of soda)

1 cup (8 fl oz/250 ml) milk

½ cup (4 fl oz/125 ml) sour cream

2 large eggs

1 teaspoon vanilla extract

⅓ cup (3 oz/90 g) unsalted butter, melted

vanilla ice cream and maple syrup, for serving

• Preheat a Belgian waffle iron. If you want to hold the waffles until serving time, preheat the oven to 200°F (95°C).

• In a large mixing bowl, combine the pumpkin, sugars, spices, and salt. Stir together thoroughly with a rubber spatula or a hand-held electric mixer. Stir in the flour, baking powder, and baking soda. The mixture will be thick and a little lumpy. In another bowl, whisk together the milk, sour cream, eggs, and vanilla. Pour the liquid ingredients over the pumpkin mixture and stir with the whisk until just combined. Fold in the melted butter.

• Whether or not your waffle iron's grids are well seasoned or nonstick, lightly butter or spray the grids for these waffles. Brush or spray the grids again only if subsequent waffles stick.

• Spoon out ⅔–¾ cup (5½–6 fl oz/170–185 ml) of batter (or the amount recommended by the waffle iron's manufacturer) onto the hot iron. Using a metal spatula or wooden spoon, spread the batter. Close the lid and bake until golden. If the waffle is hard to remove, peel it off carefully. Serve immediately or keep the waffles, in a single layer, on a rack in the preheated oven while you make the rest.

• Serve with ice cream or maple syrup, or both.

tropical coconut
and rum waffles

A sprinkling of white chocolate chips joins with the tropical flavors of vanilla, shredded coconut, and rum to give these waffles surprising flavor.

MAKES ABOUT 8 BELGIAN WAFFLES

1½ cups (7½ oz/225 g) all-purpose (plain) flour

1 tablespoon baking powder

⅓ cup (3 oz/90 g) sugar

1½ cups (12 fl oz/375 g) milk

2 large eggs

1 teaspoon vanilla extract

1 tablespoon dark rum

½ cup shredded coconut, preferably unsweetened

5 tablespoons (2½ oz/75 g) unsalted butter, melted

Chocolate-Rum Sauce (page 47)

½ cup (3½ oz/105 g) white chocolate chips

Whipped Cream (page 46)

• Preheat a Belgian waffle iron. If you want to hold the waffles until serving time, preheat the oven to 200°F (95°C).

• In a large mixing bowl, whisk together the flour, baking powder, and sugar. In another bowl, whisk together the milk, eggs, vanilla, and rum. Pour the liquid ingredients over the dry ingredients and stir with the whisk until just combined. Fold in the coconut and melted butter.

• Lightly butter or spray the waffle iron's grids, if needed. (Brush or spray the grids again only if subsequent waffles stick.)

• Spoon out 1 cup (8 fl oz/250 ml) of batter (or the amount recommended by the waffle iron's manufacturer) onto the hot iron. Using a metal spatula or wooden spoon, gently spread the batter. Close the lid and bake until the waffle is golden and set. Serve immediately or keep the waffles, in a single layer, on a rack in the preheated oven while you make the rest.

• Arrange the waffles on individual plates, pouring the Chocolate-Rum Sauce over and around the waffles. Scatter the white chocolate chips on top and garnish with whipped cream.

gingerbread waffle
ice cream sandwiches

Your kitchen will smell like Christmas when you make these waffles.
Dust with confectioners' (icing) sugar just before serving.

MAKES ABOUT 20 SANDWICHES

2 cups (10 oz/310 g) all-purpose (plain) flour

1 tablespoon baking powder

¾ teaspoon baking soda (bicarbonate of soda)

¼ teaspoon salt

1 tablespoon ground ginger

¾ teaspoon ground cinnamon

¼ teaspoon ground cloves

¼ teaspoon ground nutmeg

¾ cup (6 oz/185 g) firmly packed dark brown sugar

1½ cups (12 fl oz/375 ml) buttermilk

¼ cup (2 fl oz/60 ml) molasses

2 large eggs, separated

4 tablespoons (2 oz/60 g) unsalted butter, melted

1 quart (1 l) vanilla ice cream, softened

chopped crystallized (candied) ginger

- Preheat a heart-shaped waffle iron.

- In a mixing bowl, whisk together the flour, baking powder, baking soda, salt, spices, and sugar. In another bowl, whisk together the buttermilk, molasses, and egg yolks. In a clean dry bowl with clean dry beaters, whip the egg whites until they hold firm peaks. Stir the buttermilk mixture into the dry ingredients. Fold in the butter and egg whites.

- Lightly butter or spray the waffle iron's grids, if needed. (Brush or spray the grids again only if subsequent waffles stick.)

- Spoon out ½ cup (4 fl oz/125 ml) of batter (or the amount recommended by the waffle iron's manufacturer) onto the hot iron. Using a metal spatula or wooden spoon, gently spread the batter, stopping right before the edge. Close the lid and bake until the waffle is deep brown and set. Transfer to a wire rack to cool. Repeat with the remaining batter.

- Cut the cooled waffles into hearts. Evenly spread half of them with ice cream to a thickness of about ¼ inch (6 mm or more if you like); top with the remaining hearts. Press chopped ginger into the sides, transfer to a waxed paper-lined baking sheet, and freeze until firm. Wrap in aluminum foil to store in the freezer for up to 2 weeks.

- Arrange the sandwiches on a platter or individual chilled plates.

hot fudge sauce

MAKES ABOUT 1¾ CUPS
(14 FL OZ/435 ML)

3 oz (90 g) bittersweet chocolate

3 tablespoons unsalted butter

¼ cup (⅔ oz/20 g) Dutch-processed cocoa powder

¾ cup (6 fl oz/185 g) heavy (double) cream

3 tablespoons light corn syrup or golden syrup

2 tablespoons sugar

pinch salt

1 tablespoon vanilla extract

- Melt the chocolate and butter together in the top of a double boiler or in a bowl in a microwave oven. When the mixture is completely melted, remove from the heat and stir in the cocoa. Set aside.

- Put the cream, corn syrup, sugar, and salt in a medium saucepan and bring to a boil. Keep a close eye on the pan, as this mixture bubbles up. Remove from the heat and stir in the vanilla and the reserved chocolate mixture. Scrape the sauce into a bowl or jar and cover with plastic wrap, pressing the plastic against the surface of the sauce.

- The sauce can be served after cooling for 20 minutes. You can make it up to 3 weeks ahead, cover it well, and refrigerate. Before serving, reheat it briefly in the microwave or in the top of a double boiler.

whipped cream

MAKES ABOUT 2 CUPS
(16 FL OZ/500 ML)

1 cup (8 fl oz/250 ml) heavy (double) cream

½ teaspoon vanilla extract

1 tablespoon confectioners' (icing) sugar

- Put the cream, vanilla, and sugar in a clean bowl, preferably chilled. Use a hand-held electric mixer on medium speed or a wire whisk to whip the cream just until it is thick enough to hold very soft peaks when the beaters or whisk are lifted out. Continue beating by hand with a wire whisk if you prefer stiffer cream, to help you avoid the risk of overwhipping.

chocolate-rum sauce

MAKES ABOUT 1½ CUPS
(12 FL OZ/375 ML)

2 tablespoons firmly packed light brown sugar

1 tablespoon cocoa powder, preferably Dutch-processed

dash salt

2 tablespoons light corn syrup or golden syrup

¾ cup (6 fl oz/185 ml) milk

3½ oz (105 g) milk chocolate, finely chopped

1 tablespoon unsalted butter

1 teaspoon dark rum

½ teaspoon vanilla extract

• In a heavy-bottomed medium saucepan, whisk together the brown sugar, cocoa, salt, and corn syrup until blended. Still whisking, gradually pour in the milk. Bring the mixture to a boil over medium heat, stirring occasionally. Reduce the heat to medium-low and cook, stirring, for 3 minutes.

• Remove the pan from the heat and add the chocolate, stirring until it is melted and the mixture is smooth. Add the butter, rum, and vanilla and stir with the whisk until blended.

• Pour the sauce into a clean jar or bowl, press a piece of plastic wrap against the surface, and refrigerate until needed. The sauce can be made up to 1 week ahead, covered tightly, and refrigerated.

index